Fire

LEVEL 10

DECODABLES BY jump!

Teaching Tips

White Level 10

This book focuses on developing reading independence, fluency, and comprehension.

Before Reading

- Ask readers what they think the book will be about based on the title. Have them support their answer.

Read the Book

- Encourage readers to read silently on their own.
- As readers encounter unfamiliar words, ask them to look for context clues to see if they can figure out what the words mean. Encourage them to locate boldfaced words in the glossary and ask questions to clarify the meaning of new vocabulary.
- Allow readers time to absorb the text and think about each chapter.
- Ask readers to write down any questions they have about the book's content.

After Reading

- Ask readers to summarize the book.
- Encourage them to point out anything they did not understand and ask questions.
- Ask readers to review the questions on page 23. Have them go back through the book to find answers. Have them write their answers on a separate sheet of paper.

This edition is published by arrangement with Booklife Publishing.

North American adaptations © 2024 Jump!
5357 Penn Avenue South
Minneapolis, MN 55419
www.jumplibrary.com

Decodables by Jump! are published by Jump! Library.

Library of Congress Cataloging-in-Publication Data is available at www.loc.gov or upon request from the publisher.

ISBN: 979-8-88996-930-3 (hardcover)
ISBN: 979-8-88996-931-0 (paperback)
ISBN: 979-8-88996-932-7 (ebook)

Photo Credits

Images are courtesy of Shutterstock.com. With thanks to Getty Images, Thinkstock Photo and iStockphoto. Cover – Valeev. p4–5 – bunbok, Luciano Cosmo. p6–7 – Christian Roberts-Olsen, Protasov AN. p8–9 – Rainer Albiez, Yvonne Baur. p10–11 – Freeman Photography NZ. p12–13 – essevu, David_Johnson. p14–15 – EvdokiMari, leungchopan. p16–17 – Philip Bird LRPS CPAGB, New Africa. p18–19 – Firma V, solarseven. p20–21 – nikkytok wavebreakmedia.

Table of Contents

What Is Fire?

Fire is a chemical reaction. For a fire to happen, three things must come into contact with each other. These three things are oxygen, heat, and fuel. This is called the fire triangle.

For a fire to start, all three of the things in the fire triangle need to be present, and there needs to be enough of each of them. If one part is missing, or there isn't enough of it, then a fire cannot start.

Wildfires

Wildfires are some of the most dangerous fires on Earth. They are so dangerous because they can spread thousands of miles and are extremely hard to put out. Wildfires can happen in lots of different countries. Desert fires, forest fires, and grass fires are all types of wildfires.

Lots of things can cause wildfires. Some wildfires are started naturally because of extreme weather conditions, such as lightning. However, most wildfires are actually caused by people not being careful when they are out and about. For example, campfires or sparks from building equipment can start wildfires.

Volcanoes

A volcano is an opening in Earth's surface. It has a vent that goes deep beneath the surface where there is hot, **molten** rock called magma. When a volcano **erupts**, magma shoots up and comes out of the top of the volcano. Once magma reaches the surface, it is called lava.

Lava flows into the surrounding area. It may travel through forests or neighborhoods. While volcanoes do not produce fires themselves, the lava they spew is very hot. It can reach up to 2,200 degrees Fahrenheit. The heat from the lava can set trees or homes on fire.

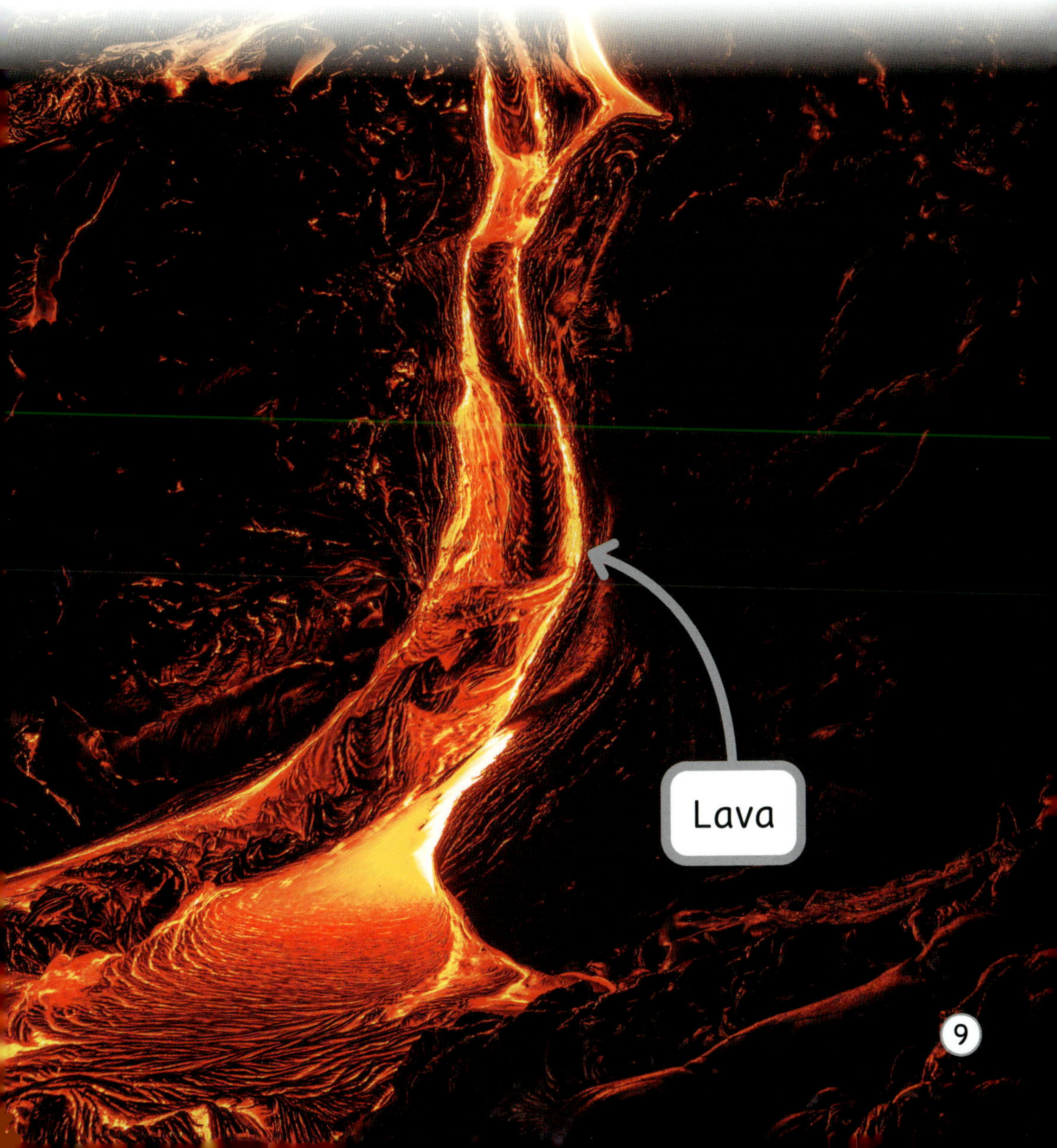

The Great Fire of London

On September 2, 1666, a small fire broke out at a bakery on Pudding Lane in London, England. The fire started to spread, and soon the whole city was ablaze. It became one of the biggest fires in U.K. history.

Without the technology we have now, the firefighters of 1666 had a much tougher job putting out the fire than we would if it happened today. To stop the fire, the firefighters used water pumps and pulled down buildings to stop the fire from spreading.

Fighting Fire

For as long as people have been using fire, they have also been fighting fire. The ancient Egyptians used a water pump that historians believe is the first example of firefighting equipment. The Romans are thought to have created the first ever fire **brigade**.

Modern Rome

As technology gets better, the way we fight fires changes. Today, firefighters have lots of smart equipment. Fire engines can hold up to 2,000 gallons of water. Fire trucks have ladders that can reach high places to help people. Firefighters also have special suits that allow them to walk through fire.

Friendly Fire

When it gets out of control, fire can be very dangerous. However, when we can control fire, we can turn it into something helpful. When it is cold, we can use heat from fire to keep us warm. For thousands of years, people have used fire to cook their food.

We also use fire for lots of things that you might not expect! Fire produces lots of heat energy and light energy. Every type of energy can be changed into another type of energy, such as electrical energy. We use fire to power huge generators that make electricity.

Power station

Transportation

Transportation has always been an important part of life. People have always needed to travel, and the energy that fire produces helps us do this. Fire became an important part of transportation in the early 1800s, when the very first steam-powered train was built.

The first steam train journey took place in 1804. Steam trains use fire to burn a type of fuel, such as coal. The fire then produces steam, which pushes the motor around. The motor then turns the wheels, moving the train.

Festivals of Fire

Fire can be dangerous, but it can also be useful. Fire is often celebrated across the planet. A festival is an event during which many people come together to celebrate a part of their **culture**. There are many festivals across the world that celebrate or include fire in some way.

One of the biggest events in the United States is **Independence** Day. On July 4 every year, Americans celebrate their independence. They light fireworks. Another festival with fireworks is Bonfire Night in the United Kingdom. People also light large bonfires. This event takes place on November 5 each year.

Fireworks

In Case of Emergency

Making sure you know what to do if there is a fire is very important. First, shout. If you see a fire, shout "fire" to let other people know. Make sure you know where all exits are so you can get out quickly if a fire starts.

Check the doors. If you see smoke coming through a crack in a door, do not open that door. Stay low! Smoke rises, so stay low so you do not breathe in too much smoke. Finally, call 9-1-1 and ask for help with the fire.

Index

How to Use an Index

An index helps us find information in a book. Each word has a set of page numbers. These page numbers are where you can find information about that word.

Page numbers

Example: balloons 5, 8–10, 19

Important word

This means page 8, page 10, and all the pages in between. Here, it means pages 8, 9, and 10.

Questions

1. What three things make up the fire triangle?

2. Where did the Great Fire of London start?

3. What is the first thing you should do if you see a fire?

4. Using the Table of Contents, can you find which page you can read about wildfires on?

5. Using the Index, can you find a page in the book about fireworks?

6. Using the Glossary, can you define what molten means?

Glossary

brigade:
A group of people that organizes for a certain purpose.

culture:
The beliefs and practices of a specific group of people.

erupts:
When a volcano violently and suddenly spews out lava.

independence:
Freedom.

molten:
Something that has turned into liquid because of heat.

transportation:
Movement from place to place, often with a vehicle.